NETWORK MARKETING
The Business of the '90s

Mary Averill, M.Ed., MBA
Bud Corkin, J.D.

A FIFTY-MINUTE™ SERIES BOOK

CRISP PUBLICATIONS, INC.
Menlo Park, California

NETWORK MARKETING
The Business of the '90s

Mary Averill, M.Ed., MBA
Bud Corkin, J.D.

CREDITS
Editor: **Andrea Reider**
Managing Editor: **Kathleen Barcos**
Typesetting: **ExecuStaff**
Cover Design: **Carol Harris**
Artwork: **Ralph Mapson**

Copyright 1994 by Mary Averill, M.Ed., MBA and Bud Corkin, J.D.

Printed in the United States of America

English language Crisp books are distributed worldwide. Our major international distributors include:

CANADA: Reid Publishing Ltd., Box 69559-109 Thomas St., Oakville, Ontario, Canada L6J 7R4. TEL: (416) 842-4428, FAX: (416) 842-9327

Raincoast Books Distribution Ltd., 112 East 3rd Avenue, Vancouver, British Columbia, Canada V5T 1C8. TEL: (604) 873-6581, FAX: (604) 874-2711.

AUSTRALIA: Career Builders, P. O. Box 1051, Springwood, Brisbane, Queensland, Australia, 4127. TEL: 841-1061, FAX: 841-1580

NEW ZEALAND: Career Builders, P. O. Box 571, Manurewa, Auckland, New Zealand. TEL: 266-5276, FAX: 266-4152

JAPAN: Phoenix Associates Co., Mizuho Bldg. 2-12-2, Kami Osaki, Shinagawa-Ku, Tokyo 141, Japan. TEL: 3-443-7231, FAX: 3-443-7640

Selected Crisp titles are also available in other languages. Contact International Rights Manager Suzanne Kelly at (415) 323-6100 for more information.

Library of Congress Catalog Card Number 93-73201
Averill, Mary and Bud Corkin
Network Marketing
ISBN 1-56052-244-5

This book is printed on recyclable paper with soy ink.

ABOUT THIS BOOK

Network Marketing is not like most books. It has a unique "self-paced" format that encourages a reader to become personally involved. Designed to be "read with a pencil," there is an abundance of exercises, activities, assessments and cases that invite participation.

This book is designed to give readers a basic understanding of what network marketing is. This book will serve as your guide as you learn how to enter and build a successful network marketing organization.

Network Marketing can be used effectively in a number of ways. Here are some possibilities:

► **Individual Study.** Because the book is self-instructional, all that you need is a quiet place, some time, and a pencil. By completing the activities and exercises, you should not only receive valuable feedback, but also practical steps in creating a viable work option.

► **Workshops and Seminars.** This book is ideal for reading prior to a workshop or seminar. With the basics in hand, the quality of participation will improve. More time can be spent on concept extensions and applications during the program. The book is also effective when a trainer distributes it at the beginning of a session and leads participants through the contents.

► **Remote Location Training.** Copies can be sent to those not able to attend "home office" training sessions.

► **Informal Study Groups.** Thanks to its format, brevity and low cost, this book is ideal for "brown-bag" or other informal group sessions.

There are other possibilities that depend on the objectives, program or ideas of the user. One thing is certain; even after it has been read, this book will serve as excellent reference material that can be easily reviewed.

Limits of Liability and Disclaimer of Warranty
The author and publisher of this book have used their best efforts in preparation of this book and make no warranty of any kind, expressed or implied, with regard to the instructions and suggestions contained in this book, nor any guarantees of income.

PREFACE

Network marketing is a business of the future. Like others, there are many pitfalls to be understood, but unlike many, there is tremendous financial potential if understood and operated correctly. Network marketing should be investigated by anyone who is interested in small business opportunities, a second source of income for their family, or the opportunity for financial independence.

Network Marketing: The Business of the '90s is a down-to-earth, real-world book, written by people who have experienced the ups and downs of this industry and who have enjoyed extraordinary success in the business. The book is designed to cover three important areas of basic information with regard to the industry of network marketing:

1. What is network marketing and why is it such an exciting, talked-about, but often misunderstood industry today?

2. What should you look for and what should you be wary of in choosing an appropriate, successful network marketing company?

3. What are the day-to-day steps one needs to take in order to become successful in the network marketing business?

Good luck in your new business venture!

Mary Averill   Bud Corkin

ABOUT THE AUTHORS

Mary Averill has both a master's degree in Education and an MBA from Harvard University. Early in her career, Mary was a banker with the Bank of Boston, where she specialized in debt and equity financing for start-up high-technology companies. She later became vice president for the First Interstate Bank in charge of corporate lending activities. Mary is an entrepreneur, having owned several businesses and been on the boards of directors of others. She has taught CEOs and entrepreneurs at the School of Management at Boston University. Involved in network marketing first in 1989, Mary Averill is now recognized around the world for her contribution to the industry in the area of teaching and training in network marketing.

Bud Corkin was a lawyer for 22 years. Early in his career, Bud served as the chief litigator for the U.S. Environmental Protection Agency. He became an Assistant Attorney General for the State of Massachusetts, and chief of its Environmental Protection Division. Later, Bud moved into private practice, and was a senior partner in a major Boston law firm. Bud maintained a large, successful law business for eleven years prior to making the decision to leave the practice of law and choose network marketing as a business.

Today Bud and Mary are recognized and ranked among the most successful network marketers in the history of the industry.

CONTENTS

1

Understanding Network Marketing

QUIZ: WHAT IS NETWORK MARKETING?

Take this brief quiz to assess your understanding of network marketing.

True **False**

☐ ☐ 1. Major corporations such as Coca Cola, MCI and Colgate-Palmolive have expanded into network marketing.

☐ ☐ 2. Highly successful people are not good prospecting candidates.

☐ ☐ 3. Network marketing is becoming the most powerful distribution method in business today.

☐ ☐ 4. You can earn income in network marketing by receiving a percentage of the income of the people you recruit into the organization.

☐ ☐ 5. The biggest drawback to network marketing is the often substantial outlay of money to set up the business.

☐ ☐ 6. Network marketing has a strong appeal for people who are entrepreneurial.

☐ ☐ 7. There are often expensive legal, financial and accounting service fees associated with network marketing.

☐ ☐ 8. Network marketing has global sales potential.

☐ ☐ 9. Person-to-person contacts are a slow and ineffective way to build a big business.

☐ ☐ 10. Network marketing is often used as a second or alternative source of income.

Answers: 1. T 2. F 3. T 4. T 5. F 6. T 7. F 8. T 9. F 10. T

NETWORK MARKETING: A PERSON-TO-PERSON PROCESS

"In the '90s, we won't go to the store, the store will come to us."

—Faith Popcorn, author, from the *Popcorn Report*

Network marketing is a form of direct selling: it is the creation of a network through which products or services are sold. It is the process of people telling other people about a product or a service, and bringing these products or services *directly* to the consumer.

The network marketing "distribution channel" develops through people inviting others into the business. Distributors thereby receive a percentage of other people's product sales in an indirect or "leveraged" manner.

Network marketing carries with it the potential for significant economic rewards for those individuals who learn how to create this kind of distribution system. A distributor begins by becoming in effect, a "store" and has the potential to build multiple "stores," much like a master franchisor.

Why is it that major corporations such as MCI, US Sprint, Coca Cola, Colgate-Palmolive, Gillette, Avon, and Fuller Brush, among many others, have become involved in network marketing?

According to a March 1992 article in *Success* magazine by Valerie Free entitled "Magic Marketing," many major corporations are finding that word-of-mouth people-to-people marketing is a powerful and cost effective approach to garnering market share.

Network marketing refers to direct selling through a network. *Multilevel marketing* is a multiple-level sales compensation plan. Sometimes the words are used interchangeably.

Direct selling, including matrix sales, multilevel marketing, or network sales, refers to direct person-to-person sales—network marketing. Right now, there are millions of people involved in direct selling, which, according to the Direct Selling Association (DSA), moves approximately $12 billion worth of products through the market annually in the United States alone. The DSA has approximately one hundred fifty corporations in its membership and recognizes approximately 5.1 million salespeople. Sales through this method in the United States last year rose by 8.8 percent. The number of people involved in direct selling has gone from 3.6 million in 1987 to over 5 million in 1992. It is enormously successful in other countries as well. According to the World Federation of Direct Selling Association, approximately $62.5 billion of product was sold worldwide through direct selling methods in 1992.

THE ORGANIZATIONAL STRUCTURE

A network marketing company normally has two essential parts: the *administrative organization* and the *distributor organization*.

The company (the administrative organization) generally has the following kinds of responsibilities:

- Market analysis

- Product research

- Product development

- Advertising

- Packaging

- Warehousing

- Shipping

- Distributor and customer service

- Distributor commission payout

- Development and management of national and international expansion

- Accounting/reporting

- Managerial reporting for administration and distributors

- Government relations

The administrative organization generally has no responsibility for the direct selling of products—that's the job of the distributor organization.

THE ORGANIZATIONAL STRUCTURE (continued)

An independent distributor generally has three basic rights:

1. To buy products at wholesale

2. To sell products at retail

3. To sponsor new distributors into their organization and, therefore, receive a commission on the sale of products by other distributors.

The following diagram illustrates how an independent distributor organization is structured:

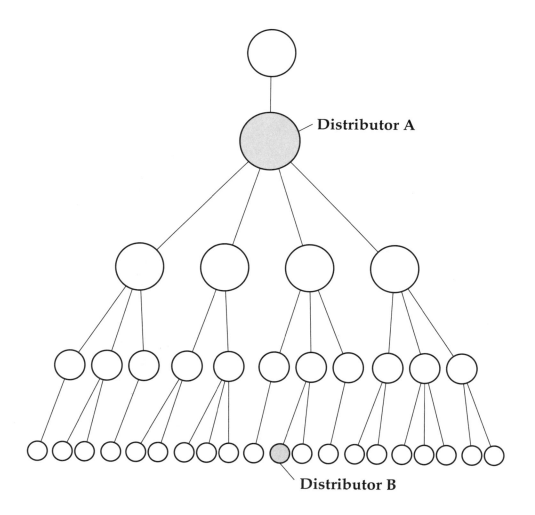

People introduce the business to others who, in turn, introduce the business to still others. Distributor A may never have met Distributor B; nevertheless, Distributor A may still be paid a percentage of Distributor B's wholesale purchases. This is known as the leverage of time. The organizational structure grows, and in time, exponential growth is possible. Normally, the administrative organization tracks relationships and productivity by computer, and then gives computer reports to distributors on a monthly basis.

The distributor's job is to:

✔ Retail products

✔ Recruit and build a distribution organization

✔ Teach, train, coach, and motivate

Since the administrative organization does not sell the products or services directly to the consumer, it is willing to pay generous commissions to independent distributors who build effective distribution channels. Network marketing companies pay distributors not only on the direct sales that a distributor makes, but also on the sales of other distributors in his or her downline organization.

THE ORGANIZATIONAL STRUCTURE
(continued)

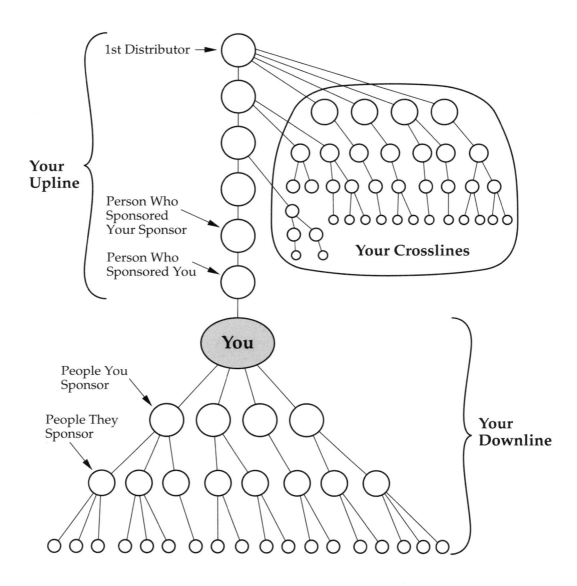

Your downline is all the people who came into your personal organization, and all the people who are linked to someone that you sponsored. Your upline is all the people to whom you are linked, all the people whose organizations you are in. Your sideline or crossline is all the people who are in your business, but not directly or indirectly linked to you. Crosslines and sidelines provide no economic reward, but may offer support in building your business. The economic reward relationship is with your upline and downline.

A LEVERAGED INCOME VEHICLE

"I would rather have one percent of a hundred people's efforts than one hundred percent of my own."

—J. Paul Getty, billionaire and industrialist

Compensation plans and organizational structures may vary dramatically, but one characteristic that all multilevel marketing companies have in common is *leverage*.

There are basically two kinds of leverage in business: 1) leverage of capital, and 2) leverage of time. In network marketing, leverage is receiving a percentage of other people's work through receiving a percentage of your downline's wholesale purchases from the company.

Many people cannot get ahead because their job or small business consumes so much time. Time leverage is one way to get ahead. Give yourself a value per hour, then fill in the blanks to find your current income cap.

$$\frac{_____}{\$/\text{hour}} \times \frac{24}{24\,\text{hours}} = \frac{\$_____}{\text{Your Current Income Cap}}$$

When the total product sales in your organization multiplied by your commission percentage is greater than what you could produce alone, you start getting ahead, and you can use that to get ahead some more.

So many people are becoming interested in network marketing because it removes the cap on income potential—with little or no capital risk.

Quiz

Yes   *No*

____   ____   1. My ultimate goal is to be my own boss.

____   ____   2. I have set a specific yearly income goal.

____   ____   3. I have established a reasonable timeline to meet my financial goal.

____   ____   4. In my answer to the equation above, I am dissatisfied with my current income cap.

(You should be able to answer yes to each question.)

MARKET TRENDS POINT TOWARD NETWORK MARKETING

We are currently experiencing the convergence of a number of trends that have dramatically enhanced the attractiveness of network marketing.

Downsizing of Corporate America

A job in corporate America no longer comes with a guarantee. In unprecedented numbers, those once solid corporations of North America, which held an unspoken contract with their employees for lifetime tenure, are now reneging. In the last few years in the United States, 2.3 million jobs have been lost and the replacement incomes are averaging 25–30 percent less.

There are thousands of highly skilled senior executives, middle managers, and sales and service-oriented individuals who are looking for jobs. These men and women are turning to small business alternatives for control over their lives. Network marketing has great appeal for them and they represent a ready pool of potential distributors.

Upturn in Entrepreneurship

Since the advent of the interactive personal computer, the world has seen an unprecedented increase in entrepreneurship. People look for small businesses because they represent the best economic return available in our society. Most people who venture into their own businesses are between 30–50 years of age, which is the current age range of our "baby boomer" population—one third of the population of North America. Women, disillusioned from attempts to break through the corporate glass ceiling, are leaving to start their own businesses in unprecedented numbers.

For those entrepreneurs looking to start a small business, network marketing offers many attractive characteristics, including low capital risk and the ease of operation.

Low Capital Requirements

Unlike traditional small business, network marketing *requires* (check any that especially appeal to you):

☐ No expensive legal, financial or accounting services

☐ No maintenance or overhead

☐ No employees

☐ No advanced education

☐ No business experience

☐ No large amount of start-up money

A network marketing business can be operated on little or no capital. Starter kits from network marketing companies generally range from about $45 to a few hundred dollars at most. Initial inventory investment can range from zero to a few thousand dollars at most.

The requirements for success in network marketing are:

✓ **DESIRE**

✓ **COMMITMENT**

✓ **ACTION-ORIENTED**

✓ **INTEGRITY**

✓ **POSITIVE ATTITUDE**

✓ **WILLINGNESS TO HELP OTHERS**

MARKET TRENDS POINT TOWARD NETWORK MARKETING (continued)

Advances in Technologies

Network marketing has not always been as smoothly operated as it is today. The industry has markedly improved its operations because of the tracking and communications capabilities of computer systems.

Voice mail, cellular car phones, and fax machines, which improve the speed and efficiency of communications have enormously enhanced efficiency in managing larger network marketing organizations.

Conference call capabilities and satellite conferences can link distributors and prospects anywhere in the world. Enhancements in shipping are allowing customers to receive products quickly, thus minimizing the need to maintain high inventories.

Globalization of the Economy

There are no territorial limits in most network marketing companies. The word-of-mouth process moves products through "circles of influence." Those "circles" have no territorial barriers, and can be used to advantage in the network marketing business. People who live in rural or depressed areas of the country can now have access to the stability of broad-based markets through network marketing. People who live in one country can do business in several countries and have an international operation without overhead.

Personal Autonomy and Freedoms

Most jobs or businesses have us tied to a boss and other employees, a fact that erodes our sense of autonomy. Network marketing is constructed with independent distributors; people there to help you because it is in their economic interest to do so.

An Aging Population

In 1990, only 4 percent of the population was over 65. Today it is about 12 percent, and by the year 2020 that figure will be approximately 25 percent. People are turning to network marketing as a second or alternative source of income, or "safety valve," for their families.

Distribution Channel Alternatives

As Paul Zane Pilzer, author of *Unlimited Wealth,* said in the March 1992 issue of *Success* magazine, "Manufacturing costs have fallen so much in the past two decades that today distribution represents 85 percent of the value of goods at retail. Therefore, the greatest opportunities in the 1990s are for those who reduce the cost of distribution."

When the cost of distribution is lowered, more of the price per unit is available to be put into quality of materials and ingredients—and to profit. Consequently, if a network marketing company chooses to have superior quality products, the cost structure allows it to be a fierce competitor relative to other companies that choose traditional retail distribution methods.

Because advertisers face increasing challenges to reach consumers, major consumer-related corporations are increasing the budget allocated to direct promotion versus advertising. Person-to-person communication is a more effective way to reach consumers.

Beyond Franchising

The Small Business Administration (SBA) estimates that within the first few years of operation, approximately 85 percent of business start-ups fail. Franchising is a viable option because the small business survival statistics are relatively good.

Many people turn to franchising because the successful franchise programs have proven products, packaging, delivery systems, and a training system, all of which enhance the likelihood of success. An individual might pay a franchise fee of $2,500–$100,000 or more, and will pay an ongoing percentage of revenue, normally between 5–7 percent. In addition, a franchisee will have a time-limited contract and, generally, a territorial limit as well. In the 1940s, when franchising was developed by the auto parts industry, it was not even considered moral, let alone good business. Later, once the food chains caught on, the popular acceptance became enormous. Now approximately one third of all retail sales in the United States are done through franchise networks.

Network Marketing

SIMILAR TO FRANCHISING	SUPERIOR TO FRANCHISING
• Significant Marketing Power	• No Franchise Fees
• Proven Products	• Little or No Capital Risks
• Proven Operations Approach	• No Territorial Limits
• Proven Training Systems	• No Contract Time Limits
• Name Recognition	• No Overhead
• Increasing Acceptance	• No Percentage of Revenue Paid to Franchisor

As a consequence, hundreds of thousands of individuals are migrating to network marketing each year, because the sophistication is growing, the technologies have made it all so much easier, and the risk reward profile is unprecedented.

P A R T

2

What To Look For
and What To Avoid

CHOOSING AMONG THE OPTIONS

It is imperative to understand clearly the potential pitfalls of network marketing. You need to be clear about what to look for and what to avoid in several important business categories. Remember as you read that there are always exceptions to any rule and you must look at a network marketing company in its totality, not just with respect to one single factor.

Check These Factors

Before choosing a network marketing company, you want to investigate the following:

- ☐ Legality of company
- ☐ History of company
- ☐ Financial strength of company
- ☐ Structure of company
- ☐ Strategic plan of company
- ☐ Quality of management
- ☐ Quality of products
- ☐ Size and direction of markets
- ☐ Timing
- ☐ Compensation plan
- ☐ Inventory requirements
- ☐ Training and support structure
- ☐ How you fit

CHOOSING AMONG THE OPTIONS (continued)

Legality of the Company

What To Look For

Legitimate business: First and foremost, get involved with a *legitimate* network marketing company, not with an illegal pyramid scheme. Although on the surface they can look alike, the following chart gives basic distinctions between what is a legitimate company and what is a possible pyramid.

ILLEGAL PYRAMID SCHEME	NETWORK MARKETING COMPANY
• Paid directly just for recruiting investors	• Paid only on product sold
• Often no product at all or product without real use or demand	• Product with real consumer demand
• Upline always makes more than downline	• Downline can make more money than upline
• Substantial capital requested ($5,000–$20,000)	• Little or no capital investment ($45–$2,000)
• Pyramids have a limited life, usually less than two years	• Company has been in business for a substantial period of time

What To Avoid

An illegal pyramid: A scheme where the products are not relevant; where money is made on the recruiting process rather than on the product. Any company that appears suspicious should be investigated as a possible pyramid.

Pyramid example #1: No Real Product
Years ago there was a famous pyramid scam in which the company was supposedly selling cosmetics. In reality, the company received money from each new recruit and gave money to the distributor for each new recruit. The company advised the distributors that it would store their products since they were not really necessary to generate commissions. Money was made by recruiting distributors who paid for the right to recruit others. It was discovered eventually that there was not even adequate product in the warehouse.

Pyramid example #2: Paid for Recruiting

You are invited into a network marketing company where a widget costs $10 wholesale and sells for $15 retail. You are told that it costs $6,000 to become a distributor. Of that, your sponsor receives $3,000 and the company receives $3,000. You are then able to sell widgets directly, and you are also able to sponsor new distributors. If you sell a widget you make $5. If you bring in a new distributor, you make $3,000. Because it is more lucrative, you spend all your time bringing in new distributors—no product moves because the product is irrelevant. In that circumstance, the sponsoring distributor is being compensated directly from your up-front fee when you are brought in, not on the products that are sold in the organization.

Avoid illegal pyramids. The SBA and your Chamber of Commerce have pamphlets that can give you greater understanding of the distinction. When in doubt, be wary.

History of the Company

What To Look For

Time in: If you have a low tolerance for risk, or even if you are just looking for a company that will be here in five years, then look for one that has already survived the blows of being in business for a while.

We are often inclined to look for a start-up, ground floor opportunity as a means of getting in on the big pay off. In reality, network marketing is a difficult business to manage from the administrative side, and the majority of network marketing companies go out of business within a few years. Find a company that has managed adversity and high growth.

What To Avoid

Ground floor, brand new, and exciting: No matter how good a product is, no matter how big a market is, if a company does not know how to manage itself for survival and growth, it won't survive. You want *proven*; you want to *avoid* ground floor, brand new, and exciting. Whether or not the company will survive should be your biggest concern after whether or not the company is legitimate—and in network marketing, the odds are dramatically against ground-floor successes.

CHOOSING AMONG THE OPTIONS (continued)

Financial Strength of the Company

What To Look For

Strong, conservatively managed finances: Ideally, you should choose a company that brings significant financial resources to a fast-growing market, and one that creates barriers to entry against the competition.

Find out if the distributors in the company which you are investigating are consistently paid correctly and on time. Ideally, find a company that separates the commission that is due to distributors into a separate escrow account, so that it does not spend the distributors' money before it is due.

What To Avoid

Cash flow problems: Because many network marketing companies are privately held, it may be difficult to obtain specific, formal financial information, but you can obtain a Dun & Bradstreet report on companies to check for history of timely or late payment of accounts payable. It is imperative that network marketing companies guard their cash flow. Particularly in high growth times, companies may experience cash flow problems due to an increase in demand for inventory. Make sure that the company you choose can manage growth.

Strategic Plan of the Company

What To Look For

Clear plan, approach to growth: Ideally, the company and its distributors should be able to articulate how, where, and when the company's growth will take place.

What To Avoid

Confusion, and no plan: If you get a muddled response to the question, "Where is the company going?", you need to look again. Without new ideas, new products, and strategies, the distributor population can lose enthusiasm; and that spells trouble for the company. If a company fails to plan, ultimately it is planning to fail.

Quality of Management

What To Look For

Ability and integrity: Because there is often a dramatic high-growth and high-income spurt in multilevel marketing (MLM), some MLM managers get involved in network marketing simply to take the money and run. Some owner/managers seek to build the business to the point where it hits dynamic growth, with the intent to shut the company down and pocket the cash rather than to reinvest in the company's or distributor's future.

Your Turn: Do Some Research

Choose a network marketing company you are considering as a business opportunity. Before joining, you need to do research and carefully scrutinize the people at the top by asking the following kinds of questions:

► What kind of people are they? _____

_____

► What is their personal integrity? _____

_____

► Are they in this for the long run? _____

► What is their commitment to taking a place in an industry, and to position their company over many years? _____

► What are their credentials, background, track records, experience, values, expectations, goals, philosophy? _____

_____

► What is their involvement with distributors, availability to all levels, and demonstration of social and environmental responsibilities? _____

_____

► Are they concerned about their distributor population? _____

_____

► What do distributors say about them? _____

_____

► How do distributors privately view them? _____

► Is there trust from the distributors about the management? _____

CHOOSING AMONG THE OPTIONS (continued)

Determine if management demonstrates high standards, the ability to operate effectively, the growth of a dynamic business, and the commitment to a lasting position in the product marketplace.

What To Avoid

Poor managers and bad character: Your first impressions and intuition should not be ignored. Investigate carefully if an owner/manager appears to have a questionable appearance, integrity or character.

If a prospective company is headed by an entrepreneur who invented the product, look closely, because often people with technical skills are ill-equipped to be good business builders, but this is not always the case.

If the company is headed by someone who is involved in both the administrative and distributor organizations, conflicts of interest exist that will make it hard to manage the organization.

Quality of the Products

What To Look For

Superiority and high demand: How do the products compete in their marketplace? If they are "me too" products, it will be a struggle to market them. If the products are clearly superior, the distributors will have a much easier time attracting new customers and new distributors. If products are just comparable in quality to others available in the marketplace but have significant price reductions, then you must consider whether, and how long, the company can survive with smaller margins. Also, determine whether consumers really want the products. Without real consumer demand, the pipeline will fill up and backfire on you.

A necessary step is to personally test the quality of the company's products by buying and using them, and reading the labels and literature. Have the products gained industry recognition? What is the reputation of the products? Do you like them? Would you use them if you were not in the business?

You want to find a company that has a commitment to ongoing product research and development, and to regular product updates based on new available research. Thus, you are looking for a company that has a clear and strong reinvestment pattern for product development.

What To Avoid

Mediocrity, pricing issues, and single product companies: The last thing that a distributor wants is a *Consumer Reports* article placing his product third in a category. In addition, unless more, good marketable products are coming soon, avoid single product companies. With single product companies, you run the risk of new competition surpassing your product, and of customers getting bored with your product. The balance of a multiple product line can greatly enhance sales and continuity of customers as well as stability in the business.

Size and Direction of the Market

What To Look For

Large, growing, preferably with emotional appeal, and preferably consumable: To avoid fighting powerful market trends, identify a strong, futuristic trend, such as health, fitness, wellness, anti-aging, personal appearance, car products, and soaps, among others. Link these trends to a network company offering superior products in a growing market. Go with the trends, not against them. Seek a broad-based, mainstream, preferably daily use market, because your distributor population will be mainstream. Never underestimate the psychological and market power of broad-based trends.

What To Avoid

Stable or niche markets: Even large markets are not good if they have peaked, because they will not excite or drive distributors or customers. Be careful of those interesting, but small, niche markets. They just are not big enough to sustain a large body of distributors over time. Be concerned about durable goods; where the consumer buys once and seldom or never buys again in a market.

CHOOSING AMONG THE OPTIONS (continued)

Timing

What To Look For

The beginnings of dynamic expansion: It is said that "timing is everything." While it may not be everything, it is a major critical factor. Identify what stage of business the company is in. Affiliate with a company which is in or about to begin a high-return stage—that time in a company's life in which the growth is going to be extraordinary. For distributors who capture that moment, the return will be extraordinary.

What To Avoid

Too early: If a company is new, it may be exciting due to its newness and potential for high growth. But you need to allow the company to prove that people will buy the products again, and that the company can manage the cash flow as it grows. Start-ups have numerous risks inherent in them: product risks, management risks, financing risks, etc. If it is truly a significant opportunity, the company will be around long enough for you to capture much of the upside sales, while avoiding the downside risk of a failed company.

Too late: If a company has not experienced growth for some time, and has not changed strategies in order to grow, it may be difficult to build an organization because there simply is not enough excitement inherent in the situation. If a company has been around for a long period of time without periods of fast growth, there may be underlying reasons why growth will not take place.

Compensation Plan

What To Look For

Potential for extraordinary return: Compensation plans can look complicated and confusing at first. A compensation plan must have the capacity to pay a worthwhile income for your productivity. With some plans, the income potential is minimal. A simple way to determine economic potential is to review how well the leaders who have been in the business for a period of 1–5 years are doing. For example, have they been able to go into business full-time? A "yes" is an indicator that the plan probably has holding power to keep attracting players long-term.

Also, make sure that the compensation plan pays "deep enough" in terms of levels of marketing groups. When you train and coach people, you should be compensated once they are successful, instead of having them "roll out" below your payout levels. Find out whether the people at the top of the business make extraordinary incomes. This is a key motivator to the sustaining of your downline distributors and attracting new ones. The larger the potential for extraordinary return, the higher the likelihood of attracting into your business skilled and effective people who have been successful in other areas.

What To Avoid

No long-term leaders, and too much payout: There is probably a flaw in the compensation plan if there are *no* extremely successful people within an organization. If a company has no leaders who have been around for 3–5 years, it is because either the money rolls out below them, or because they can't make money in the first place.

Avoid any company where the distributor begins discussion about the business by telling you about the compensation plan. The promise of wealth should be in the context of a stable, growing company that produces marketable products. A marketing plan can be ill-thought out and created in a matter of hours. By itself, or as the lead item, a marketing plan does not make a good, stable business. For example, "Our company pays out 7 breakaway levels at 8 percent and a total of 65 percent of the wholesale dollar." Ask yourself: "Can the company operate on the 35 percent, or will they be out of business before I receive my 65 percent?" Percentages are less important than the long-term stability of the company. If a company speaks about its marketing plan first, there may be little else of substance behind it. Such a company may operate similar to a pyramid, moving quick money instead of growing a steady, stable business.

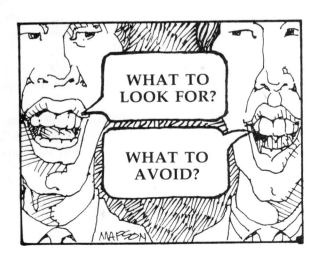

CHOOSING AMONG THE OPTIONS (continued)

Inventory Requirements

What To Look For

No requirement: Distributors should have the right to choose the level of inventory that they wish to carry. Preferably, the company has a system that does not require the distributor to invest any or much capital into inventory. Often the product can be drop-shipped directly to the consumer or to the distributor within a period of days.

What To Avoid

Front-end loading: Companies whose marketing plans are "front-end loaded" need careful scrutiny. For example, if a higher title can be bought, or if products can be purchased *for less* by acquiring a significant amount of inventory—like $10,000 or more up front—you need to be careful. Problems can arise if a person buys a lot of product, puts it in the garage or basement, and does not sell to a consumer. A few months later, when the commission checks have been paid on these products, the person may want to send them back to the company for a refund. This can create a crisis for the cash flow of the company and it can create an unhappy new distributor. Having a lot of inventory in the pipeline but not sold through to a consumer can eventually undermine the financial viability of a network marketing company.

Training and Support

What To Look For

Lots of resources: You are looking for a situation in which the basics of the business can be learned readily. Ongoing, effective meetings and trainings are essential to the individual distributor's and downline's success. Ideally, the company and distributor network have communication tools such as voice mail and teleconferencing for continual communication and involvement.

Uplines should be actively committed to their downline's success and capable of helping you. Quality tapes and manuals are enormously helpful. Investigate the tools and people available to learn the business. Who will your upline be? Are they successful? Will they help you?

What To Avoid

No commitment to training or support: Training gives a structure for downline success. You are like the president or CEO of your own network marketing activity; you are the leader of your own downline organization, and you will only be as successful as your downline. Duplication is the process by which your business will grow. A simple business duplicated well among many people brings success. Avoid organizations that downplay training, or that do only satellite meetings and never have live meetings. They will not succeed as well, or as fast.

How You Fit

What To Look For

Your own commitment: You are a critical piece of this network marketing puzzle. Find a company and a product line that you can be proud of and that you can see yourself staying committed to over time. Without your long-term commitment and consistent actions toward building the business, no one—no company and no upline—can make you successful.

Success will *not* be determined by whether or not an individual has a sales personality, a specific education, a business background, or an outgoing personality. The essentials are instead: a positive attitude, persistence, and a willingness to learn and to work. This is a people business. Successful distributors enjoy people and enjoy helping others to succeed.

What To Avoid

Misfit: If you just do not feel good around the people in the company, or if you can not see yourself using or selling the products, the company you are investigating may not be the right match for you. Look closely before saying "no," because products often grow on people.

Give yourself some time; often someone new to network marketing begins the business with a status concern: "Is this beneath me?" He or she later develops prosperity and the love of helping others and becomes a staunch network marketing advocate. We often tell people that we had status issues too until we started to make more money than most CEOs in North America.

What To Look For and What To Avoid

Do this quick check to see how well you remember the "look fors" and "avoids" of network marketing. Compare your answers with the authors'.

	Look For	Avoid
1. A company with leaders who want to teach you the business and has training materials from which to teach.	_____	_____
2. A company with a single product.	_____	_____
3. A company that wants you to buy-in to a higher level, a "front-end load."	_____	_____
4. A brand new, start-up company.	_____	_____
5. A company that will pay you directly for recruiting people who have not yet bought or used any product.	_____	_____
6. A company that pays only on products sold.	_____	_____
7. A network marketing company with a good, nonconsumable product in a niche market.	_____	_____
8. A company that can spell out its growth strategy to you clearly.	_____	_____
9. A company with proven leaders and managers who have long-term commitments to distributors.	_____	_____
10. A company and a product line that you can be proud to represent.	_____	_____

Answers: 1. Look for, **2.** Avoid, **3.** Avoid, **4.** Avoid, **5.** Avoid, **6.** Look for, **7.** Avoid, **8.** Look for, **9.** Look for, **10.** Look for.

P A R T

3

Five Steps to Network Marketing Success

THE FIVE-STEP PROCESS

"If you don't know where you are going, you won't know when you have arrived." This old adage holds as true for business as it does for day-to-day living. By following this five-step process, you will have all the tools and gain the confidence you need to become a network marketing success.

Five Steps to Network Marketing Success

STEP 1:   **CREATE YOUR ATTITUDE**

STEP 2:   **WRITE YOUR VALUES, DREAMS AND GOALS**

STEP 3:   **GAIN THE BASIC KNOWLEDGE**

STEP 4:   **UNDERSTAND BUSINESS FINANCES**

STEP 5:   **BUILD YOUR PROSPECT LIST**

STEP #1: CREATE YOUR ATTITUDE

Develop a Positive Attitude

A persistently positive attitude is critical to success in the network marketing business.

Because you attract people to yourself first, then to the products or the business, a positive attitude is essential. Without a positive attitude, you are less appealing to be around, and you cannot be the attractor that you need to be.

As in all small businesses, effort must be spent before rewards are achieved. To sustain yourself, a consistently positive attitude may make the critical difference between falling out of the business too soon, and making it all the way to financial independence. You must like and believe in yourself. If you don't, why should others?

LIST YOUR WINNERS

List five positive factors that you count on to keep an upbeat attitude:

1. _____

2. _____

3. _____

4. _____

5. _____

Beware of Dreamstealers

"Dreamstealers" abound as you start your network marketing business. There will be well-intentioned friends or family members who believe and feel the need to tell you that "it can't be done" or "you're crazy." You need to protect your positive attitude. Once you hold steady, those dreamstealers could choose to become a part of your downline. Your belief and your attitude can make all the difference, so it is important to check in on yourself regularly.

Handling Your Dreamstealers

Complete the following exercise:

My Possible Dreamstealers	*How I'll Handle Them*
Name: _____	Option #_____
Name: _____	Option #_____
Name: _____	Option #_____
Name: _____	Option #_____
Name: _____	Option #_____

Options for Handling Dreamstealers

Option #1 Invite them to look for themselves.

Option #2 Ask them to pay my bills if I don't follow this income producing option.

Option #3 Think of them as an educational challenge that will take time.

Option #4 Know that they are who they are, love them anyway, and go on.

Option #5 Cave in . . . give up my dream because they said so.

APPLY BASIC PRINCIPLES IN YOUR LIFE

A positive attitude is a learned skill; it should be continuously developed by looking at each situation as an opportunity, and viewed in a positive light.

A positive attitude creates a positive life. Once the basics of your products and your business are understood, then your success or failure rests in large part on the management of your self-esteem. People buy from you because they like you. This applies equally to the marketing of automobiles, insurance, and the network marketing of a business. A very interesting fact is that people will not like you more than you like yourself.

Therefore, to be successful you must like yourself. This can be accomplished often times by taking stock of your assets and affirming over and over, "I like myself," in writing and verbalizing. Sound silly? Maybe so, but it works.

Exercise: My Daily Affirmations

Do not underestimate the power of positive thinking. In the space provided below, list three affirmations to boost your self-esteem and attitude.

1. _____

   _____

2. _____

   _____

3. _____

   _____

Transfer these affirmations to 3 × 5 index cards and keep them with you. Look at them often and read them aloud to yourself.

STEP #2: WRITE YOUR VALUES, DREAMS AND GOALS

Determine What Is Important to You

Before you start any new endeavor, it is useful to articulate for yourself what you value most in your life, to remind yourself about what's missing, and what you want to accomplish.

This is not always an easy process but it is always a useful one. Often we become frustrated because our day-to-day reality is not in alignment with our underlying basic values. If our day-to-day actions are in harmony with our values, then we have a much greater potential for happiness.

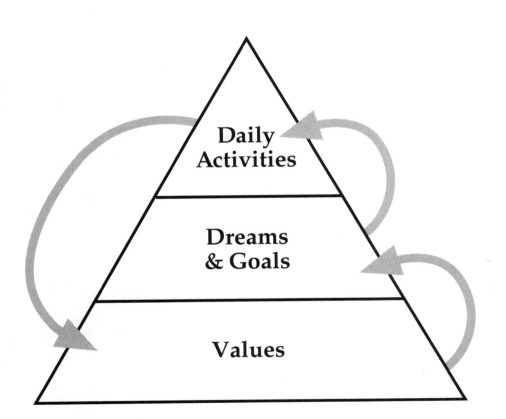

WRITE YOUR VALUES, DREAMS AND GOALS (continued)

Reestablish Your Values

Often people try to live their lives by doing a lot of tasks, without ever having a long-term direction. This is absolutely unsatisfying. Our values are our cornerstones. When starting a new endeavor, it is wise to revisit our values because they are the underlying framework for our lives. Once we have articulated what is important to us, we can decide, at the more detailed level, what our goals and tasks should be.

Key Values

Place a check mark by the 10 values most important to you.

☐ Competence	☐ Innovation	☐ Productive
☐ Contributor	☐ Integrity	☐ Selflessness
☐ Excellence	☐ Intellectual Growth	☐ Self-Sufficiency
☐ Fairness	☐ Leadership	☐ Sincerity
☐ Family	☐ Neatness	☐ Spiritual Growth
☐ Financial Security	☐ Organized	☐ Stability
☐ Frugality	☐ Perseverance	☐ Thoughtfulness
☐ Giving	☐ Personal Growth	☐ Tolerance
☐ Hard-Working	☐ Physical Health	☐ Tranquility
☐ Honesty	☐ Playfulness	☐ Truthfulness
☐ Humility	☐ Positive Attitude	

Identify Your Values

Write your three highest values:

1. _____

2. _____

3. _____

Define Your Dream

They say that in network marketing, 98 percent of the business is *why* you are doing it. Our dreams are our Whys. Why do you want this business? Why will you sacrifice to become successful? Articulate your dream for yourself—it will go a long way in helping you to become successful.

What is your dream? _____

_____

_____

_____

_____

_____

Now write the sentence or phrase that excites you to action, and that will go into your daily planner each and every day to help you to be more effective.

_____

_____

_____

WRITE YOUR VALUES, DREAMS AND GOALS (continued)

Write Your Goals

No significant achievement happens without goals.* Deciding what we want may be a lifelong process, but goal-setting can speed up the process. Often the difference between setting and not setting goals is the difference between working smart and just working hard.

To succeed, think in terms of results. Before you set your goals, identify your strengths, weaknesses, your needs, and understand your values.

Successful people make two decisions in their lives. The first is related to goals. They decide on a goal and a time they will achieve it. The second decision that they make is what price they are willing to pay for achieving their goals. Remember, the price always precedes success. The bigger the price you are willing to pay, the bigger the success you will enjoy!

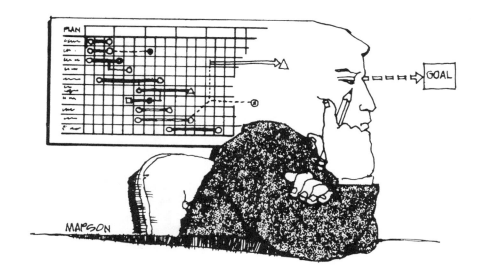

*For more information, order *Goals and Goal Setting* by Larrie A. Rouillard. Menlo Park, California: Crisp, 1994.

Goals

It is not enough to state vague goals; for example, "make more money," or "get ahead in life," or "go back to school," or "expand your business." Take it one more step: be specific.

Be specific.   **1.** *6 months,*   **2.** *1 year,*   **3.** *3–5 years*

Professional

1. _____
2. _____
3. _____

Personal

1. _____
2. _____
3. _____

Financial (salary, earnings, investments, possessions)

1. _____
2. _____
3. _____

Residential (buy, sell, expand, improve)

1. _____
2. _____
3. _____

Spiritual/Attitude

1. _____
2. _____
3. _____

Educational

1. _____
2. _____
3. _____

Physical

1. _____
2. _____
3. _____

STEP #3: GAIN THE BASIC KNOWLEDGE

As you start your new network marketing business, you need to become knowledgeable about the products, the company, the compensation plan, and the industry.

Know Your Products

The single best way to learn about your products is to *use* them. If you are serious about the business, buy all of the products if your company has a moderate product line, or buy the key products if you have a broadbased product line. Then migrate through the entire product line as soon as possible. This is necessary in order to tell people what each product smells, looks, feels, and tastes like. That way you can share the benefits of the products *from your own experience*. Your belief level will go up once you are knowledgeable about the products. Use the company's products *exclusively* whenever possible so that a visitor to your home does not see a competitor's products and lose confidence in your belief level.

Listen to and read all available material on your products. Ask your upline lots of questions about the products until you feel knowledgeable and comfortable.

Know Your Company

Read the company brochures and listen to any company tapes and videos. Talk to distributors. Visit the company if possible. Find out about those who own and operate the company, what their background is, what their philosophies are in the business, and how they view the distributor segment of the business. A business reflects the character and intentions of the people at the top, so ask questions.

Know Your Compensation Plan

How is the plan guiding you to make money? What is the plan telling you to do to make money? Do not assume that you know how to make money in this business—listen to where the plan tells you to concentrate your efforts. Then do it. Also, find out where people get stuck in the plan. Most people do not really understand their own plan. Ask questions of your upline until you get it and can, therefore, explain it to others, *simply*. Ask your *successful* upline what the plan is telling you to do and *not* to do. Simplicity is a good test of understanding in every aspect of the business.

Know the Industry

Ask questions of others who have been in network marketing in order to understand the trends and to understand who the network marketing competitors are, what their strengths and weaknesses are, and how to handle them.

One of the most useful sources of knowledge is your own upline. Call them all, tell them you are very interested and excited about the business and ask if they could give you some hints. Then take their advice, tell them you took it, and return for more. If you return for more but do not take the first advice, your upline may be less open to you in the future.

Of course, the greatest teacher is experience. Take action, then assess what works, and what doesn't. Tape yourself on the phone, video yourself if you give a group presentation, and ask for feedback whenever possible. Do two-on-ones with your upline and watch and listen to how they do the business. Go to trainings and meetings whenever there is a senior person in your area. Although MLM is a simple business, the complexity comes in the relationships with people; you should not expect to be as skilled at the beginning as you will be after the experiences of both success and failure to guide you.

STEP #4: UNDERSTAND BUSINESS FINANCES

Understand Accounting Processes

Forming a corporation to start a network marketing business is not usually necessary. A sole proprietorship or a partnership is a sufficient structure unless you have special tax or organizational circumstances. With regard to product liability protection afforded by the corporate veil, most network marketing companies have an umbrella insurance policy for their distributors that protects them from product liability legal actions. Starting your network marketing business as a corporation creates extra expense, time and reporting requirements that dampen the attractiveness and ease of entry. And since this is a business of duplication, the next person will do what you did. Thus, you want to keep it simple wherever posible.

An important benefit of network marketing is that for little or no capital you can create a small business which allows you to begin to take certain appropriate tax deductions.

As you start your business, it is a good idea to have a discussion with an accountant about tax deductions applicable to your style in running the business, as well as about the latest IRS deduction rules. You might be able to deduct a portion of your home, computer, car, travel, etc.

A bookkeeper or accountant can assist in setting up a simple accounting system. Bookkeepers are generally less expensive. Maintain a separate bank account and separate credit card for your business to avoid mingling business and personal expenditures, which would make for an accounting nightmare.

Eventually, adding a simple software accounting system to your computer may be useful. But do these kinds of things *after* you are in action and have decided that you like and will stick with the business.

Be Realistic about Money Matters

To avoid wasting money, determine to buy *only* what is necessary for the business. The multitude of available support materials can eat up cash and not advance your business one step. Listen to your upline about what is *important* to buy, and about what can wait.

For people who are new to small business, it is important to understand the reality of the difference in cash flow between a job and a self-funded small business. In a job, a certain, regular amount of money comes in every week, or two weeks or month, no matter what people do or do not do, until or unless they get promoted, fired, or leave. Then, at the end of the year, there is, perhaps, a minor increase in that amount, based on merit or cost of living.

In your own start-up, you put in what seems like endless hours of effort and time to get the business off the ground with little return for the time invested in the early stages. The distinction here is that you are not paid for effort, you are paid for productivity. And there is much to be done in laying the groundwork before a business becomes productive in the sense of moving enough product through the market to make significant money.

CASE STUDY: You Have to Start Somewhere

One distributor tells that when he started his business, to his wife's dismay, he worked hours upon hours his first month, and was very proud to call her when his first check came in. "Honey, we made 875 this month." Then he paused and said, "The only problem is that the decimal is after the 8." His wife later grew very happy about the business, as his income soared to triple what he had *ever* earned before.

Make sure that you can live for some time with income from some other job or other source until the cash flow begins to come your way in your new business. Ask your upline to be realistic with you about the time frames and income levels you can expect. You do not want to find yourself in a cash-flow bind just when your business begins to blossom. It is wise to replace current income before jumping into network marketing full-time because there are ups and downs in the initial stages of the business.

UNDERSTAND BUSINESS FINANCES
(continued)

A Dollar Saved Is a Dollar Earned

It is important to be able to distinguish among the many spending opportunities that are available to you. Some are true business necessities, some will be appropriate in the future, and some probably never will make good business sense. Mark each of the following spending opportunities and compare your answers with the authors'.

	BUY NOW	NOT NOW	MAYBE NEVER
1. An accounting package to put your business' accounting information on your personal computer.	_____	_____	_____
2. A personal computer for your accounting package.	_____	_____	_____
3. A limo for moving people to meetings.	_____	_____	_____
4. Key products for your own use and for sale to others.	_____	_____	_____
5. An office outside the home to impress others.	_____	_____	_____
6. Basic training tapes and materials.	_____	_____	_____
7. The complete video package that claims to market the business.	_____	_____	_____
8. Limited quantities of recruiting materials that have been recommended by your upline.	_____	_____	_____
9. Five hundred product/company brochures.	_____	_____	_____
10. Ten product/company brochures.	_____	_____	_____

Answers: 1. not now **2.** not now **3.** maybe never **4.** buy now **5.** maybe never **6.** buy now **7.** maybe never **8.** buy now **9.** not now (maybe never) **10.** buy now

STEP #5: BUILD YOUR PROSPECT LIST

Who Do You Know?

A key tool in the network marketing business is your prospect list. In order to be efficient and effective in getting your message to as many people as possible, you start by putting together a list of names and phone numbers of everyone who should hear about your products, and about this extraordinary business opportunity.*

There are some people whom you will be hesitant to call. Be sure to put them on your prospect list. We call this our "chicken list" because we are too chicken to call them, probably because we think that they are too successful to listen to what we have to say. Ironically, they are also the ones most likely to succeed because they have been successful in the past; so be absolutely sure your chickens are on your list!

Before you start calling your prospects, order three-way (conference) calling from the telephone company ($2 to $3 per month). With this aid you can talk with a prospect and an experienced upline distributor at the same time. Therefore, chickens on your list can be called with someone who is successful already in the business and who is not scared of your chicken because it is not their chicken.

*For more information, order *Prospecting: The Key to Sales Success* by Virden J. Thornton. Menlo Park, California: Crisp, 1994.

Prospect List

PRODUCT		OPPORTUNITY
1 _____	Friends	1 _____
2 _____	Family	2 _____
3 _____	Business	3 _____
4 _____	Acquaintances	4 _____
5 _____	Neighbors	5 _____
6 _____	Referrals	6 _____
7 _____	Service Providers	7 _____
8 _____	People you used to know:	8 _____
9 _____		9 _____
10 _____	• school	10 _____
11 _____	• former jobs	11 _____
12 _____	• old neighbors	12 _____
13 _____	• former spouse	13 _____
14 _____	• yellow pages	14 _____
15 _____		15 _____
16 _____		16 _____
17 _____		17 _____
18 _____		18 _____
19 _____		19 _____
20 _____		20 _____
21 _____		21 _____
22 _____		22 _____

Rules:

1. Do not edit your success.
2. Retail supports recruiting; recruiting supports retail.

After you have learned the basics of recruiting and role played with your upline, you'll start to make calls. You may wish to get on the phone with your upline and let them make the presentation or invitation to a meeting.

If you want to build a successful business fast, generate a long list of people, the longer the better—150–300 names if possible, although the names may not occur to you all at once. Many people feel at first that they do not have a large "circle of influence" or "do not know anyone." Many shy, private people have become enormously successful in network marketing, but they had to first get focused about the number of people they have known over the years even in a passing way. In this business those with the biggest prospect lists win. Not because they know so many people, but because they decided to make the world a prospecting environment.

Prospect List (Insert to Daily Planner)

DATE CON-TACTED	NAME	PHONE NUMBER	COMMENTS

Keep this list simple: names and phone numbers, and keep it nearby with you always. If you are serious about the business, you will start to continuously add names as you meet people at the office, shop, grocery store, or laundry.

Whatever you do, avoid keeping names on little pieces of yellow paper or on cards. Your prospect list is your most important practical tool in the day-to-day operations of your business. Every opportunity prospect should be told about the products, and every retail customer should be told about the opportunity.

A key factor in network marketing is that it has little or no capital investment. Thus, people get involved, wanting the upside income that is possible. However, if they are operating their network marketing business as a hobby, it's little wonder that they do not achieve the incomes they've dreamed about. Even though there is not a capital risk, one needs to treat this as a real and serious business with huge national, perhaps international, potential. So, operate it like a business. Keep a prospect list and take action by calling prospects every day to build a group of people interested in the products and the business. This does not mean that you need to do this full-time at all. It simply means that when you do it, you need to do it full tilt. This kind of business can be done successfully ''part-time'' but not ''spare time.''

BECOME A NETWORK MARKETING LEADER

The single best way to become a leader in network marketing is to do the business energetically until you find what works, and then have an unbending commitment to pass along what you've learned.

To teach, train and coach your downline organization, focus on three basic concepts:

> **#1: This Is a Business of Duplication**
>
> **#2: Teach the Basics**
>
> **#3: Be Available**

This Is a Business of Duplication

The power of this business is leverage, in which you get a percentage of other distributors' efforts and corresponding geometric growth in the organization by enabling people to do a simple process and teach it to others. People will learn that process primarily *by watching you*. In reality, they will not listen much to what you say, they will learn from what you *do* and *don't do*. Therefore, you need to be doing the business exactly the way you want others to do it, or else you will have a trail of ineffectual activity down numerous lines of people. So, the first rule in managing your downline is, *do what you would have others do*—lead by example.

In fact, managing a downline is a misconception. Once the downline is initially developed, we begin to spend time talking with distributors, advising them, analyzing them, mistakenly believing that we will not have to get back on the phone and continue to build our organization through recruiting and retailing. This is a major mistake that almost everyone makes. Instead, *show them* what they should be doing, by staying glued to the phone yourself, and by always bringing new people into the business. When you have new people at the meeting each week, your downline *sees* you doing this and then learns to do it themselves.

What is the best example in life that you have seen of duplication?_____

_____

Is this a good analogy to the network marketing business?_____

Why?_____

Teach the Basics

What each new distributor and what each senior distributor actually needs is *the basics*. Teach and remind them of setting goals, making enough calls daily, building rapport, handling objections, and closing. Remember, repetition is a good teacher.

Signs and Symptoms

Test your awareness of you and your downlines' progress. Place a check mark in the box by the appropriate statement. If there are any marks in the "symptoms" column, be sure to schedule time to discuss your assessment.

EARLY SIGNS OF SUCCESS	EARLY SYMPTOMS OF A DROPOUT
☐ Asks lots of questions	☐ Asks few or no questions
☐ Writes down goals	☐ Does not write down goals
☐ Starts thinking of prospect list immediately	☐ Does not make an adquate prospect list
☐ Loves it when upline calls	☐ Says "What can I do for you?" when upline calls
☐ Calls prospects and upline daily	☐ Makes few if any calls
☐ Is very coachable, really listens	☐ Says or thinks "I'll do it my way."
☐ Has a dream	☐ Has no burning desire

On the following page is a checklist of items that are basic to the business and are critical to your downline.

The "15 Basics" Checklist for Coaching Downline

For instructions on using this checklist, refer to pages 53 and 54.

	#1		#2		#3		#4		#5		Comments
	C	S	C	S	C	S	C	S	C	S	
#1 Goals											
#2 Use of Product											
#3 Prospect List											
Daily Calls											
#4 Knowledge											
#5 Inventory											
#6 Training											
#7 Tapes											
#8 Personal Volume											
Retail Customers											
#9 Recruiting/											
Role Playing											
#10 Objections &											
Closing											
Role Playing											
#11 Three-Way Calling											
#12 Honoring Update											
#13 Staying Connected											
#14 Increasing Self-Esteem											
#15 Maintain A Positive Attitude											

Using the "15 Basics"

The "15 Basics" checklist is an important tool to use to keep yourself and your downline on track. Use the checklist for yourself as you review each numbered item. When you have a downline, use this checklist with them as well. As you review each item with your downline, place a check mark in the boxes under the C (coach) column and S (student) column.

> **This is a very effective tool—use it often.**

#1. Goals: Are your goals tangible and exciting? (Without goals, why go through the tough times?)

#2. Use of product: Do you use all the products and love them? (Without belief in the products, they will not get far.)

#3. Prospect list/Number of daily calls: Do you have a *long* prospect list? Are you making numerous calls per day? (Nothing replaces massive action.)

#4. Knowledge about products and company: Are you learning all about the products and the company? (Knowledge breeds confidence.)

#5. Inventory: Do you have inventory appropriate to your goals? (Do you have an inventory level that could be sold in one month?)

#6. Training: Do you go to meetings and trainings regularly and avail yourself of every training tool possible? (The more training, the more chance of success.)

#7. Tapes: Do you know about the latest tapes? (Much of our learning and recruiting occurs through audio tape, because tapes are efficient.)

#8. Personal volume/Retail customers: Do you have an appropriate level of personal sales volume coming in part from retail customers? (This is the backbone of your business.)

#9. Recruiting: Do you know how to recruit? (Role playing with your upline helps build skills.)

#10. Handling objections and closing: Do you know how to handle objections? Are you afraid to close? (Again, role playing is a powerful teaching tool.)

THE "15 BASICS" CHECKLIST (continued)

#11. Three-way calling with upline: Do you have three-way calling on your phone? (Three-way calling allows you to learn how to make calls *live* in real time, first with your upline, and later you teach your downline while you are on the call with their prospects and they can listen in.)

#12. Honoring upline: Do you honor your upline? (You do not need to love or even like your upline. But it is important to treat them with respect and keep communication open.)

#13. Staying connected with the organization: Are you connected to your upline, to your downline, and to corporate? Do you go to meetings and gatherings regularly? (Do not underestimate the power of staying connected.)

#14. Increasing self-esteem: Are you working on increasing your self-esteem? (We can all always increase our self-esteem. This is important in part because this is a business of attracting other people and others are attracted to those who like themselves.)

#15. Maintaining a positive attitude: Do you monitor your basic attitude? (Once the business information is understood, the biggest challenge is to keep a positive attitude.)

Be Available

The final area that you should keep your eye on in working with your downline is that you "be available."

What that means is that you have a way to get messages when you are not present, and that you answer those messages quickly. It means that you do three-way calls with your downline. It means that you are present at all meetings. It means that you give your downline the feeling and the knowledge that they are important to you and that their issues and concerns matter.

P A R T

4

The Day-to-Day Business

RETAILING PRODUCTS AND GAINING CUSTOMERS

Everyone in a legitmate network marketing organization does some retailing. How much you retail depends on your goals. For instance, if you are using this to make a car payment or pay some bills, then your time can be spent mostly or completely on retailing.

If, on the other hand, you want the income from this business to replace your current income or you want financial freedom, then retailing will become a smaller segment of your time, just as CEOs of international businesses do not often do all of the direct sales of their company's products. The larger incomes in network marketing come from *leverage*, from doing some retailing and then by recruiting and teaching many other people how to use the products and sell them.

Building a Retail Customer Base

Retailing is a simple process. The following steps will bring you your retail business:

#1: **Build your prospect list.** Continuously build a prospect list with people who you think will enjoy your products and your business.

#2: **Make calls.** Call someone and, with *enthusiasm*, tell them briefly about your business and/or products.

#3: **Invite someone to a product presentation.** Suggest getting together to show the products at no obligation. Schedule a meeting or visit on neutral ground or on your territory (never at their house or office).

#4: **Make the presentation.** At the meeting, highlight the *benefits* of your products. People need to learn why they will be better off with your products.

#5: **Close.** Ask for their business. Assume that the person wants to experience these great products. If you have done your job well enough in teaching them about the *benefits* of the product, they should be practically asking how to get started on the products.

#6: **Mention the business opportunity.** At some point, mention that there is a business opportunity available. Those distributors who forget to do this may one day find that their retail customer is in someone else's organization.

RETAILING PRODUCTS AND GAINING CUSTOMERS (continued)

Maintaining Satisfied Customers

Once you have made a sale, serve that customer, and that volume, month after month. Tell your customers that you will call on a regular, periodic basis. Then, use a tickler file and call, periodically, to see if they are happy, if they have any concerns, what they are ready to reorder, etc. Suggest additional products for them to try. Remember, service is the key to success in retailing.

If your company has an automatic re-order option, get your customers onto it. The customer is often happier on an automatic re-order system, feels better taken care of by the company, and you are relieved of involvement in day-to-day handling.

RETAILING IS IMPORTANT

You Get to Know Your Customers:
It keeps your hand on the pulse of the market, what the customer likes, wants, needs and what changes or preferences are occurring in the market.

It Duplicates Volume:
Large volumes come from many people doing a little. Teach your entire organization how to do some retailing simply, and efficiently while building the organization, thereby reproducing small volumes in large quantities.

Remember, the people who decide to do network marketing in a major way, in time, become like master franchisors . . . they spend most of their time teaching others how to run a successful, duplicatible small business.

RECRUITING TO BUILD AN ORGANIZATION

Some people have concerns about recruiting such as being afraid to approach people or not wanting to be a salesperson with their friends and neighbors. In reality, we are all recruiters. We are recruiting to our business, to ourselves, to an idea or to a way of life almost all of the time. Recruiting is simply *inviting* someone else to look at something that you have, that you love, and that you believe in.

The same is true for any business—in order to grow, you need to be in a recruiting mode to attract and teach the best talent so that your organization can thrive under your leadership and theirs.

Let's look at how to recruit key players. In network marketing we can *not* determine who the winners or big players will be by knowing their education, business background, age, sex, race, or nationality. None of these are determining factors for success in this business. Instead, the determining factors are:

WINNING FACTORS

1. **Positive personality**

2. **Willingness to learn**

3. **Burning desire**

4. **Consistent persisting action**

Prospecting and Inviting

Most recruiting is accomplished on the phone because that is a very efficient way to sift for interested people. You can invite your friends, acquaintances, or prospects to any of the following:

- Your house
- A hotel meeting
- A luncheon meeting
- A conference call
- Someone else's house
- To listen to a tape

RECRUITING TO BUILD AN ORGANIZATION (continued)

The purpose of your call is to allow the person to see enough possibility of something good for themselves that they decide to come along and investigate. That is all you need to accomplish. Do not try to give someone the entire business over the phone. This is nearly impossible, and is the wrong objective for the call.

You may also invite someone to look at your business when you are at the gym or the grocery store, or after a business meeting. Again, the only purpose of your conversation is to get them scheduled to be in front of the entire presentation, so that they can really understand what it is you have to offer. Do not over-discuss the opportunity, just invite—with enthusiasm! Let their curiosity do its job of getting them to the presentation. Too much said satisfies the curious nature and stops people from coming.

The words we use represent less *than 10 percent* of our effectiveness in recruiting. So, what's the other 90 percent? See below:

Seven-Point Recruiting Strategy

#1: **Build Relatedness**

#2: **Show Enthusiasm**

#3: **Carry a Positive Posture and Stance**

#4: **Hold a Vision of Success**

#5: **Create Interest and Curiosity**

#6: **Focus on Contributing**

#7: **Keep Up Your Volume**

#1: Build Relatedness

Always get related first (in both warm and cold markets). In other words, build a rapport, a relationship of trust.

Your prospects must feel good about you and have a relatedness or relationship with you before they can begin to hear what you have to say. You may find out that the timing is not right for someone.

There are three basic ways to get related:

▶ **Compliment** (not flatter) **your prospect.** The compliment must be sincere.

Examples:

- *"You'd be perfect for this business."*
- *"You were always a pleasure to work with."*
- *"Nobody has more integrity than you."*
- *"I want your opinion because I think so highly of you."*

Make sure that you feel real about the compliment.

▶ **Find something in common.** The acronym F.O.R.M. (**F**amily, **O**ccupation, **R**ecreation, and **M**oney) is a helpful way to remember how to find commonality.

Examples:

- *"Are you a skier?" "A runner?" "A weight lifter?" "A reader?" "A walker?" "A tennis player?" "A golfer?"*
- *"What do you do?"*
- *"Do you love what you do?"*
- *"Does that make you as much money as you want?"*

Remember, you want your relating to be real and to make sense. You will become more proficient with relating over time.

RECRUITING TO BUILD AN ORGANIZATION (continued)

▶ **Show interest and excitement in the other person.** When you are interested in them, you are interesting to them.

Examples:

- *"Wow, that's terrific . . ."*
- *"How interesting, tell me more . . ."*
- *"What's important to you in life?" "What's missing?"*

#2: Show Enthusiasm

Enthusiasm excites. Enthusiasm generates interest and creates curiosity. Enthusiasm sells!

Remember: A sale is a transfer of enthusiasm.

Examples:

- *"I'm involved in a new and exciting business . . ."*
- *"I've found something that you* have *to see . . ."*
- *"I've got something that I can't wait to show you . . ."*

If you are dull, you are not attractive, and that is not what you are trying to communicate.

#3: Carry a Positive Posture and Stance

Posture and stance are a major key to success. You need to hold several background beliefs to have the right strength and stance. Some of these are belief in the:

- ✔ Extraordinary nature of the business opportunity

- ✔ Superiority of your products

- ✔ Value and importance of your business

- ✔ Direction you are going and that the other person should come along

✔ Urgency of developing your business now

✔ Business and that it is appropriate for the prospect

✔ Ability you have to bring this person to success in your business

Examples:

- *"This is too important to wait . . ."*

- *"You're busy? Cancel it . . ."*

- *"No, I'm not going to send you some literature; what I will do is send you an audio tape—but I'm sending it out overnight mail only if you promise me you will listen to it the day you get it and we'll talk the next day. Is that a promise? You have to hear about this . . ."*

- *"This is by invitation, I'm reserving you a seat. So tell me now if you're not going to be there. If there is a possibility that you'll cancel, let's not make the appointment. I'll be there for you. I'm putting it in my calendar . . ."*

- *"That's what I thought at first too. Think about it this way . . ."*

#4: Hold a Vision of Success

You need to hold a vision of success in your mind for your prospects.

Envision the person you are talking to:

▶ Signing the distributor agreement

▶ As a success in your business

▶ Happily involved in spending their money on what they want and being free to go where they want during the day

RECRUITING TO BUILD AN ORGANIZATION
(continued)

#5: Create Interest and Curiosity

People come to a meeting out of curiosity. People don't come when they think they know what it is. Do not say too much when you invite—do not satisfy the curiosity. This is not done out of deception; it is rather with the intent to let the person see the entire presentation intact, which is nearly impossible to do over the phone.

Examples:

- *"Wait 'til you see this. This situation is extraordinary."*

- *"It's too important to talk about over the phone."*

- *"There is a fascinating presentation that takes about an hour. It's on the cutting edge."*

#6: Focus on Contributing

Each time you interact with someone, remember to keep your eye on that person's well-being. The question becomes "What's good for that person?" not "Is the person going to make me money?" When you are focused on contributing to other people, the business and the income is a natural outgrowth.

Keeping an attitude of contribution is not easy. It is one of the ironies of this business.

A Parable

There is an ancient formula for turning lead into gold. You melt lead in an iron pot, stirring slowly, all the while *not thinking* of the word "gold." In the past, alchemists would stir and ask, "now what is that word I may not think of? Gold!"— and the spell would be broken.

Think of the business as a gift for your prospect. Do not think of your prospect as money for yourself. If you can think of your prospect's happiness and best interest, your own money will come.

7: Keep Up Your Volume of Contacts

Volume of contacts is critical to success. If you dream and hope but do not take regular and consistent *action*, nothing is realized in this business.

You need to talk with several people each day to generate enough activity to grow a real business instead of a hobby.

You are sifting the population to find those few people who are entrepreneurial and willing to work for their dreams. If you want to create a large business, we recommend you make at least twelve contacts per day, so that you develop and keep activity in process always. The more people you talk to, the bigger your business will grow. Other kinds of recruiting businesses, like personnel placement, insurance, and stock brokerages require significantly higher contact-per-day numbers, and they have less residual income potential.

VOLUME
IS THE KEY
TO SUCCESS!

P A R T

5

Prospecting

HOW TO PROSPECT

The more you like someone, the higher they should be in the order of who you should talk to first. You want to make sure that you have a *written* prospect list of not less than one hundred fifty to three hundred people. This list will consist of two main types of people: warm and cold.

Your Prospect Lists

Warm List

1. Family and friends

2. Business and personal acquaintances

3. Other people with whom you have connections

4. Referrals

5. List of names where you have a relatedness—school, clubs, organizations, etc.

6. Friends' lists—corporate, organizational

Cold List

1. "Walk and talk" around town, meeting new friends

2. Meeting strangers—while doing daily activities

3. Utilizing other people's circle of influence

4. Advertising

Remember:

The purpose of the contact is to invite the person to a meeting.

HOW TO PROSPECT (continued)

✔ Do not underestimate your existing circle of influence (warm list). This is statistically likely to produce the most results for you.

✔ Get good at asking for referrals, so that you never run out of warm market prospects.

✔ Work in the warm market until you have called everyone in your warm list. Do not jump to walking and talking or advertising too fast, because the statistics show that you need to make more contacts in your cold market than in your warm market. You will eventually get good at both markets.

Types of Prospects for Initial Contact

There are numerous types of prospects, each of which might merit a slightly fine-tuned approach, such as:

▶ Close relative

▶ Not-so-close relative

▶ Active, close friend (in touch recently, know each other well)

▶ Inactive, close friend (friend, but haven't been in touch in a while)

▶ Inactive, former friend (used to have a close relationship, but haven't been in touch in a long time)

▶ Active acquaintance/personal (seen recently or often, but do not know well)

▶ Active acquaintance/business

▶ Cold call: related in some way (school, club, etc.)

▶ Cold call: unrelated (phone book, etc.)

▶ In-person stranger

▶ Answers to ads

▶ Long distance (various types of relationships)

THE REFERRAL APPROACH

You can also take an indirect approach in your conversations, asking people who they know who might be interested in a business; results are that they refer someone to you and/or that they speak up about themselves.

The Basic Conversation

We recommend that you tend to lead with a conversation about the business instead of the products during times of high growth, and when you are first building the infrastructure of your organization, because it tends to be more efficient in sifting for entrepreneurs. Leading with the products is also a legitimate alternative.

Sample Conversation:

- *"How are you?" "How are the kids?"*

- *"How's business?"*

- *"How's the job?"*

- *"Would you be interested in a new business opportunity or possibility?"*

- *"Would you be interested in a second source of income for your family?"*

- *"Would you be interested in earning some extra income?"*

- *"Would you be interested in the potential for financial freedom? I'm involved with a business that you have to see."*

THE REFERRAL APPROACH (continued)

The Referral Conversation

"I'm with a company that is in a high growth mode now. I'm an executive," and "I'm doing some recruiting today. The top people in my business make more money than most people can think of." "I'm looking for a few key people to work with in this geographic area. I'm looking for two or three people that might come to your mind who might appreciate a call like this, who might be unhappy where they are, not making enough money, or are just looking for an extraordinary business alternative. I will treat them courteously, and if they are interested I will invite them to a formal business preview as a guest—if they are not interested I will take up no more of their time."

When you get a name the following is a good example of what to say:

"Shannon, Kim Lee gave me your name and said that you were quite entrepreneurial and a go-getter (or whatever was said about the person). She thought that you would be interested in hearing about a business opportunity. I'm with a company that went from $ _____ to $ _____ revenue."

If they say they are interested themselves, you can follow with:

"You say you might be interested—tell me a little bit about yourself," or "I've got slots on Tuesday at 2 P.M. or Wednesday at 4 P.M., or, better yet, why don't you come to our business preview on _____ at _____ Hotel. Just come to the registration desk and say you are my guest, otherwise they will charge you. If you say you are coming, I will be waiting for you."

Create Your Own Beginning Dialog

Who are you pretending to talk with? _____

Relationship to you?

☐ relative ☐ friend ☐ acquaintance ☐ cold

How will you begin? _____

_____

_____

_____

What are you asking them for (or asking them to do)? _____

_____

_____

_____

Ask for an appointment. _____

_____

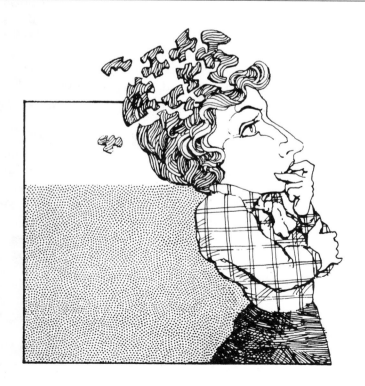

DOING THE PRESENTATION

In making your formal business presentation, do what has *proven to be successful* for others. Locate the successful people in your upline organization and learn everything you can from them. Watch how they do the presentation, and with their permission, use that same presentation. If they have developed materials for you, use those. Later on, once you really know the business, put your own personality, style, and emphasis in and change accordingly. But, initially, stick with tried and true methods and experience.

If you are too shy to do a presentation yourself do not worry. Ask your upline to do it for you, or to help you. You can also often plug into existing presentations in hotels or phone calls. Or you can use a video or audio tape if necessary. Learn how to present as soon as possible because network marketing is a leadership business.

Points to Remember

The following points are important to remember about a presentation:

▶ *Be enthusiastic:* Your enthusiasm is contagious—the more you have, the more they get.

▶ *Keep to a one hour limit:* Do not spend more than one hour on the presentation; people cannot listen much longer. If you have done a good job, people will stick around to get more information after the formal presentation. Plan your presentation well; remember concise is effective.

▶ *Speak to prospect's hot button:* Tailor the conversation toward what is important to your prospects, and what might be missing in their lives currently.

▶ *Close:* Be sure to actually, specifically invite the person to become a distributor. Most sales are lost because the prospect is never asked if they are interested in buying.

DON'T LET OBJECTIONS DAMPEN YOUR ENTHUSIASM

UNDERSTANDING AND OVERCOMING OBJECTIONS

Whenever you introduce someone to a new concept or a new product, and particularly, to a new business, that person will have objections. Objections are normal. Do not be surprised or scared by them.

What are objections really? Objections are generally one of five things:

- A *request* for more information. For example, "Is this a pyramid?"

- A legitimate *concern*. For example, "I'm not a salesperson."

- A *smoke screen* hiding the real, hidden concern. For example, "I'm too busy."

- A *polite putoff* because they have not seen the value for themselves of what you are saying. For example, "I'll think about it."

- A *test* of your belief and knowledge level. For example, "You can't really make any money doing this."

Once you understand objections, and understand that they are part of a legitimate investigative process, you can learn how to overcome them. There is a saying that the average sale is made after the fifth objection, and the average salesperson quits after the second objection.

What you need to do is educate your prospect, taking care of their concerns, matching their goals in life with what you are offering. Persist, until the person gets what they need to make an informed decision.

The following are a few examples of ways to respond to an objection. There are countless other ways that are not given here and that will occur to you as you gain experience.

Objection: *"It's too expensive."* (Remember, expect a price objection whenever marketing anything, because it is always more expensive than if they bought nothing.)

Response: (The key here is to make sure that the person perceives more value in what is offered than in the money it costs, so talk about the *benefits* to the individual.) *"Haven't you usually found that when it comes to quality you get what you pay for?"*

UNDERSTANDING AND OVERCOMING OBJECTIONS (continued)

Objection: *"I'm too busy," or "I don't have any time."*

Response: *"I know how you feel. I felt exactly the same way. (Tell your story here.) That's why I invited you. What I have found was that successful people tend to be busy people. The wonderful thing about the business is that you can get it started and growing on a few hours a week."*

Objection: *"I don't have money."*

Response: *"That's why I got involved in this business. There is little or no capital risk. Unlike other businesses, it does not take a large investment to get the chance for large financial return."*

One of the interesting things about objections is that they are quite limited. Your organization will give you guidance about handling these limited number of objections.

Objections can come fast and look hard, but if you stick them out and stay with an educational approach, giving the facts as you know them, your business should stand up to scrutiny and satisfy the questioning nature of all good prospects.

People have a right, and perhaps a duty to themselves, to ask a lot of questions if they are going to commit their time and energy to something. Remember, objections are limited, just satisfy them, outlive them and you will succeed.

Overcoming Your Own Objections

1. What is your biggest concern or objection before participating in this business?

_____

_____

2. What would relieve that concern or handle that objection?

_____

_____

3. So, what actions will you take?

_____

_____

CLOSING THE SALE

Closing is simply asking for a decision. Nobody likes to make decisions because decisions create the potential for being *wrong* and for failing. Thus, the natural inclination is to "study" or "think about it," or just forget about what you're offering them. So, if you don't ask for a decision, a person won't make one.

People do not like to be "pushy." But please remember that you are not powerful enough to make someone do something that they do not want to do. Your job is to make it easy and less painful to say "yes" when they want to go for it.

Closing, or asking for the decision, will call up hidden objections and will help your prospect get closer to the true thoughts and feelings about the business. Many people in this business say that they have five to ten people "thinking about it." But, the reality is that they actually stop thinking about it when they have left the room. So you need clarity and completion, as does your prospect.

We close all the time in this business; for example, we close:

- To come to a meeting
- To sign a new distributor
- To purchase products
- To come to a training

Do not talk past the moment when your person is ready to decide. Many people keep on persuading beyond the "moment of yes," and then that moment never comes again.

CONCLUSION

Network marketing is not a complex business. Unlike most businesses, there is very little capital risk. You do not have to analyze it as much as you would if big money was at stake.

With little or no capital risk, the questions become simple: Is this the company I'd be proud to be associated with? Are the products able to capture an appropriate segment of a market? Can I believe in them? Will I enjoy doing the business on a day-to-day basis? All of these are answered simply by trying—experiencing both the products and the business.

A convergence of trends is making network marketing stand out as a business today. The downsizing of corporate America, the aging of the population, the reduction of effectiveness of advertising as an approach to the consumer, the ease and speed of communications technology, the increase of entrepreneurship, and many other trends have positioned network marketing for a staggering boom in the next decade.

Network marketing is fast becoming the single most powerful distribution methodology in business today, both in the United States and worldwide. Ultimately, however, the underlying reason for the extraordinary attractiveness of network marketing is lifestyle—the potential for person, economic, and time freedom.

One of the most appealing aspects about this business is that it provides a level playing field—productivity, not capital or politics, matters. Anyone can get involved, and if network marketing is done well enough and long enough, anyone has a chance to become prosperous.

Network marketing is not an easy road; you have to work hard. But have you ever seen anything real or worthwhile where you did not have to work? You need to choose your corporate vehicle carefully, and then remember that if you want a big business, you cannot treat this like a hobby. The one "flaw" in the industry is that we do not have a capital investment, and so people often lose track of the need for intense, regular, business-like effort to achieve significant success.

If you choose this industry, you are about to embark on a wonderful adventure in business and in personal development. There is no replacing or even aproaching the economic potential that comes from creating a source of leveraged income. And, ironically, there is no way to help other people grow a people-oriented business without becoming a bigger person yourself.

Good Luck and Happy Network Marketing!

OVER 150 BOOKS AND 35 VIDEOS AVAILABLE IN THE 50-MINUTE SERIES

We hope you enjoyed this book. If so, we have good news for you. This title is part of the best-selling *50-MINUTE*™ *Series* of books. All *Series* books are similar in size and identical in price. Many are supported with training videos.

To order *50-MINUTE* Books and Videos or request a free catalog, contact your local distributor or Crisp Publications, Inc., 1200 Hamilton Court, Menlo Park, CA 94025. Our toll-free number is (800) 442-7477.

50-Minute Series Books and Videos Subject Areas . . .

Management
Training
Human Resources
Customer Service and Sales Training
Communications
Small Business and Financial Planning
Creativity
Personal Development
Wellness
Adult Literacy and Learning
Career, Retirement and Life Planning

Other titles available from Crisp Publications in these categories

Crisp Computer Series
The Crisp Small Business & Entrepreneurship Series
Quick Read Series
Management
Personal Development
Retirement Planning